Hide the Treasure

Written by Lisa Thompson
Pictures by Craig Smith

A treasure chest was in the sand.

"Treasure for us!" said the pirates.

"We will hide it," said the Captain. "Lift it up."

"Come on," he said. "We will hide it over here."

The chest was very heavy.

They had to pull and pull.

"We will hide it here," said the Captain.

They dug a big hole in the sand.

"No one will see the treasure now," they said.

"One day, we will come and get it!" they said.